The Four Color Personalities for MLM

The Secret Language For Network Marketing

Tom "Big Al" Schreiter

For information, contact:

Fortune Network Publishing
PO Box 890084
Houston, TX 77289 USA

Telephone: +1 (281) 280-9800

ISBN: 1-892366-34-7

ISBN-13: 978-1-892366-34-4

DEDICATION

This book is dedicated to network marketers everywhere.

I travel the world 240+ days each year. Let me know if you want me to stop in your area and conduct a live Big Al training.

http://www.BigAlSeminars.com

Get 7 mini-reports of amazing, easy sentences that create new, hot prospects.

Sign up today at:

http://www.BigAlReport.com

Other great Big Al Books available at:

http://www.BigAlBooks.com

TABLE OF CONTENTS

PREFACE

Many networkers have asked me for a simple explanation of the four personalities. Hippocrates started the idea around 400 BC, and over the last century, many psychologists and speakers have taught and expanded on his original work.

Unfortunately, most of this work is too deep and detailed, and gets boring very quickly. Plus, the average networker wouldn't find it very usable. For example, some systems analyze people by having them take a 25+ question test. While it is more accurate than just observing, a 25+ question test is not very practical to give to prospects before you speak to them.

This book is designed to help you:

1. Quickly identify which personality types your prospects are.

2. Know the exact words to say to those prospects in their secret language so your message is received more easily and with more rapport.

Now, for the students of endless detail, this isn't your book. There are plenty of psychologists and gurus who love this topic. There are textbooks and volumes written on this subject.

For network marketers who want to have more rapport and connection with prospects, this is a quick and easy way to learn not only how to talk to prospects more effectively, but also what not to say to prospects so that you don't sabotage your message.

— Tom "Big Al" Schreiter

Four things you should know about this book.

#1. Psychologist warning.

If you are a psychologist, you will probably hate this book. It won't be entirely accurate according to Hippocrates or some of the great psychologists of the 20th century. But we are not trying to psychoanalyze prospects. We don't want to put them on a couch and counsel them. All we want to do is take a little bit of the science of personalities to help us talk in a way that our prospects will understand.

For the academic purists reading this, we are not contradicting the centuries of personality studies. We are using just a tiny bit so that we can talk to prospects and they can understand us. No psychologists' jobs will be harmed in the reading of this book.

#2. Forget the rigid systems you might have learned before.

If you have studied personality profiling before, you know the temperaments: phlegmatic, sanguine, choleric and melancholic. Ugh. That is difficult to remember. So forget what you have learned in the past while reading this book. Sit back, relax and enjoy.

This book is an **easy-to-learn** shortcut, so that we instantly know exactly what to say, and exactly what to do when we meet a prospect. It is not practical to survey a prospect's feelings, have the prospect fill out a questionnaire, analyze the answers ... and then say your first words. We just need something to guide us so that we can talk in that prospect's natural language.

Think of this as the "lite" version of all those volumes of research.

#3. Don't take this personally.

I am going to describe the personality types. You will naturally recognize yourself in one of the personalities. All of the personalities have **good points** and **bad points**.

When I describe the bad points of each personality, don't take it personally. I don't want you to run me over in the parking lot the next time you see me.

So for the next few chapters, relax. Just pretend that all of the bad points of your color personality apply to other people.

#4. I am going to use a lot of exaggeration.

Not every prospect is going to have all the exaggerated characteristics that I will describe. However, I will exaggerate because it will be easier to **remember**.

All we really want is an easy-to-remember method to recognize prospects, and instantly know how to talk to them in their natural language.

So I will use lots of exaggeration here and a few bad jokes. Don't take it too seriously. It will simply help us remember the differences in people more easily.

Does this look familiar?

Have you ever talked to a prospect and had this happen?

1. The prospect desperately needed your product. (And you just happened to offer this product to your prospect.)

2. The prospect desperately wanted your opportunity. (And you just happened to offer your business to your prospect.)

Then, at the end of your presentation, the prospect says, "No."

What happened? What went wrong?

Does this seem strange to you?

This mystery costs you time and money. So when would be a good time to fix that problem? How about right now?

Let's review.

If your prospects need your product and opportunity, and then you offer your product and opportunity, and then … they say, "No" … the most obvious explanation is:

They don't understand you!

When you talked to them, it was like you were speaking a foreign language. They just didn't receive your message the way you intended.

Let me give you an example:

1. You have a great product or service.

2. You have an awesome upline support team.

3. The company founder "walks on water" … when it is frozen.

4. Your company offers a terrific training program.

5. Your compensation plan pays out massive amounts.

6. The company offers trips and cars.

And all of that stuff doesn't matter. It is not important.

Huh?

Yes, all of that stuff doesn't matter.

Need proof?

To prove this, take your distributor kit and PowerPoint presentation and fly to a small town in Portugal. Now, you don't speak Portuguese. And, they don't understand your language.

Now, start giving presentations.

* Would it matter if your upline team was supportive?

* Would it matter if you had a company bonus car program?

* Would it matter if your company paid 3% more on level 3?

* Would it matter if your company founder walked on water ... when it was frozen?

* Would it matter if you had a 74-page research report from the University of North Carolina saying your product was wonderful in a double-blind study?

* Would it matter that your scientist could beat up their scientist?

Everything that you thought was important doesn't matter, does it?

Your attitude, your motivation, your product, your research, your service - none of those mean a thing and won't help you build a business until you learn:

The skill of speaking Portuguese.

Until you can speak your prospects' language - in this case, Portuguese - none of the things you consider important in our business mean anything to our prospects.

If you can speak your prospect's language, then everything is easy. Your prospect will instantly **see what you see**, and you will be happily conversing with a friend who understands you.

What will happen when you speak the language of your prospects?

* Your message will quickly go to their hearts and to their minds.

* You can say a few sentences and you will know they will come to your opportunity meetings.

* With a few words, many of your prospects will want to join your business, even before they hear the name of your company.

And the good news is ...

The secret languages are easy to learn. You will only have to learn a few words in each of the four different languages. That is the easy part.

When you say the proper words, it feels like you are a blood brother or blood sister, you are "joined at the hip," you are walking hand-in-hand on the way to a common vision ... it feels wonderful.

And the bad news is ...

Learning the secret language isn't the skill. The real skill is knowing which secret language the prospect understands.

Yes, you will have to quickly determine **which** of the four secret languages your prospect understands. That is the skill that will make your career soar.

This will be easy to do. Once you read the examples in this book, you will quickly know the right language to use in almost every encounter with a prospect.

The "yellow" personality.

All you have to do is remember one word. This one word describes the yellow personality.

What is the word?

"Help."

That's it. The yellow personalities will do more for other people than they will for themselves. Sort of sounds like someone's mother, doesn't it?

These people are professional helpers. They live for the chance to be of assistance. It makes them feel good to help.

When a neighbor is sick, who comes to their home and brings food? Who nurses them back to health? Who takes them to the doctor?

Yellow personalities.

I keep a picture in my mind of a yellow personality. I visualize a 50-year-old grandmother, long hippie dress, flowers in her hair, serving cookies to the grandchildren, while singing "Kumbaya" and other folk songs.

Exaggerated? Of course, but if you can remember that picture you will never have to memorize the attributes of a yellow personality.

You will find many yellow personalities as:

* Massage therapists

* Kindergarten school teachers

* Fund-raisers

* Nurses

* Social workers

* Charity volunteers

* Ministers

* Counselors

* Customer service representatives

* Caregivers

Why? Because they enjoy careers that help people.

Yellow personalities are professional huggers. They love to hug people. I bet you have an aunt or cousin who, when she meets a stranger, comes up to the stranger and gives that stranger a huge hug. And the stranger says, "Oh, I feel like I have known you all my life. Here is all my money."

When a new road is being built through the woods, they are the ones hugging the trees saying, "Please don't hurt the trees."

Everybody loves the yellow personality. And everybody trusts them, too.

You'll know when you have met a yellow personality. Not only does she give you a big hug, but the next day you get a thank-you card in the mail. The card says, "Thank you for being my friend." And when she signed the card, did she put a little dot over the "i"?

No. There was a little heart over the "i" and smiley face stickers everywhere. That is the yellow personality.

Now because the yellow personalities are always helping people, they are **not** interested in your compensation plan, the overseas trip for top leaders, or the scientific reports on your patented products.

They are more interested in how your product or service can help other people. If the network marketing company cuts the compensation plan by 50%, the yellow personalities will say, "Oh, that's nice. Our bonus checks will only be half as much and that money will probably go to help poor people or a pet shelter somewhere."

Yellow personalities are fine with that scenario. They are only interested in the business as a means to help other people.

They want to know how your product helps stop the suffering of people in pain, how your product saves money so that young mothers will have more money for baby food, and how your skin care can help the self-image of a shy teenager.

They are so happy just helping people.

Yellow personalities make great network marketing leaders. People are naturally attracted to them because of their integrity, their honesty, their willingness to help, and their missionary spirit. Once they are convinced of something, their missionary spirit overcomes their fear of rejection, and they become self-motivated for their cause.

You seldom see yellow personalities in the front of the room motivating the attendees. They are not the type to be giving orders or telling other people what to do.

You normally see them in the back of the meeting room because they like to support the function instead of being seen as the star. They organize the registration, put out extra chairs, supply refreshments, and make sure the heating and air conditioning are kept at the proper temperature so everyone is comfortable.

But that does not mean they are not good leaders. They just lead differently.

Remember Mother Teresa? Remember Mahatma Gandhi?

They were great people who led by their personal examples. They didn't preach their philosophies to the masses. They simply lived a dedicated life of service and people followed them.

Everyone loves the yellow personalities. They are so friendly, so helpful, and so pleasant to be around.

The yellow personalities are easy to notice. They don't overdress. They are more comfortable in sandals and casual wear. They are not out there to impress people or to be seen as better than someone else.

Soft-spoken, polite, and with a leisurely pace, they go with the flow of life and fit in everywhere.

Yellows find it almost impossible to say "No" to any request. They find it easier to say "Yes" than to explain why they want to say "No."

But don't be pushy with the yellow personalities. Just because they are soft-spoken doesn't mean you can bully them into doing what you want. They want to be helpful and serving, but they don't want to be bossed around.

Even cartoon characters can be yellow.

Remember Cinderella? Yes, she was nice, kind, wanted to help people. A great example of a yellow personality.

Usually the tooth fairy and good fairy godmothers are yellow personalities too.

Many Disney princesses are yellow personalities.

Remember Charlie Brown from the cartoon strip, *Peanuts*? He always wanted to be helpful to everyone around him. But his friend, Lucy, was definitely **not** a yellow personality!

Marge Simpson, Homer Simpson's wife, is certainly a yellow personality that you can remember. She puts up with all the mistakes and drama in her family with that cheery attitude, and just wants to help everyone be happy.

Homer Simpson's neighbor, Ned, is a yellow personality. He has that jovial personality and just wants to help people and make them happy.

(Homer Simpson? No, he is **not** a yellow personality.)

Casper the Friendly Ghost was yellow. In his cartoons, all Casper wanted to do was make friends. Yellows make the best friends.

Oh, how about Big Bird from the children's television show, *Sesame Street*? Not only was Big Bird a bigger-than-life yellow personality, he also had bright yellow feathers.

And finally, there's Elmo. This well-known *Sesame Street* character was loved by everyone. No one hated Elmo. (Although there is a rumor that fellow cast member, Oscar the Grouch, harbored a deep sense of jealousy over Elmo's popularity.)

The yellow personality behavior.

They're laid-back, mellow, they hate to say "No" to a request, and they tend to talk softer and slower.

Because they don't want to disappoint people, they smile, avoid conflict, and are easy to get along with.

Remember though, their primary motivation is to **help** other people.

Let's see if you can predict a yellow person's behavior in this example:

Imagine that the yellow personality enters a large banquet room. There are large round tables, some with many happy, laughing people, and one table where a person sits by himself.

At which table will the yellow personality sit?

The table with only one person, of course. The yellow personality will put an arm around the lonely person and say, "You need a friend."

Yellows are first to help, first to volunteer, and want to make sure everyone is happy.

Have you ever experienced this?

You sit down with a friend, and your friend brings you hot tea and cookies, offers to massage your neck because you look stressed, and asks about the health of your close family members.

Yes, that is a yellow personality.

Feelings?

Yes, you can describe the yellow personalities as people with feelings who are focused more on relationships. While working on a big-picture project, they will work hard to make sure everyone gets along to move the project forward.

This is in contrast to some of the other personalities that would measure production and set goals and standards for achievement.

Yellows are great at relationships.

So what is the downside to the yellow personality?

Some people look at yellow personalities and say they are indecisive, wishy-washy, can't make up their minds. Maybe we could look at it this way instead.

Yellow personalities don't like forcing their opinions on other people. They want someone to make a decision and they will support that decision, as long as it is reasonable.

For example, you get 12 yellow personalities in a conference room. One yellow says, "Time for lunch."

The next one says, "Where should we eat?"

The next one says, "I will eat where you like to eat."

The next one says, "I will eat where everybody else agrees to eat."

The next one says, "We should form a committee, but we are not authorized to form a committee."

The 12 yellow personalities are going to starve!

Do yellows make great leaders?

Absolutely.

They are a pleasure to their upline. Why?

The yellow personality doesn't like to complain. If there are problems, the yellows don't want to criticize and moan about the problems. They simply want to help people.

So no complaints are passed upline. The yellows gladly take care of their own problems, and their downline problems. They are good at this. Because they are patient and understanding, other people feel their empathy and love to work with them.

Also, the yellows have no ego that will get in the way of their relationships with their downline. No ego means less conflict and less stress. Yellows are just nice people.

Yellows are great listeners. This is natural because they care about people.

Yellows are dependable and oh-so-patient. This makes them great team players, as everyone knows they can depend on them.

So how can I use the yellow language when talking to the yellow personalities?

The only word you have to remember is:

"Help."

Now, you are fluent in the yellow language. Easy, wasn't it?

If you can't think of what to say, simply throw the word "help" into your conversation, and you will communicate much better with the yellows.

When talking to the yellows, consider focusing on these points in your presentation:

* How your business opportunity **helps** young mothers to stay home with their babies.

* How your company has a charity that raises funds for the **needy**.

* How working at home **saves** the environment by reducing commuting pollution.

* How working at home gives more time for the family, to build stronger **relationships**.

* How the nutritional product **helps** people save their livers from those evil pharmaceutical drugs.

* How the products **help** grandmothers by giving them the energy to take their grandchildren to the zoo.

* How the skin care **helps** teenagers get rid of their acne so that they have a better self-image, go back to their classes in high school, go on to university, become doctors, and help save starving children in the world.

What is less important to the yellows.

As polite people, we should only talk about what the other person is interested in. So out of respect for the yellows, we won't spend a lot of time talking about:

* Compensation plan details.

* Winning a company trip as a top producer.

* Big bonus checks.

* Company sales and growth numbers.

This is pretty easy. Now, why didn't they teach us this in high school? We would have been a lot more polite and effective when talking to the yellow personality.

Help, help, and help some more.

When I do a live workshop, I ask all the yellow personalities to raise their hands. Then, I say to the attendees,

"Look closely at all these yellows raising their hands. Everybody loves these people. They are the kindest, most helpful people on the planet. So during the upcoming break, go to them and ask them for a loan of $1,000."

Everyone laughs, but now we understand the yellow personality.

When you really appreciate that the other person is a yellow personality.

As you walk to your car in the parking lot, a stranger jumps out and says, "Hands up! Give me all your money!"

You answer, "But I don't have any money. I just spent the rest of this week's paycheck."

The stranger replies, "Oh, that is so sad. Can I lend you a few dollars to help you through the rest of the week?"

A great time to be held up by a "yellow" criminal. I guess that is why most criminals aren't yellow. They just can't make a living with that soft, caring heart.

Or, while driving home, you don't pay attention to the traffic, and you drive your car into the car in front of you. It is a major accident. The owner of the car in front of you says, "Oh, did I back into you? Are you hurt? Let me give you a hug!"

Yellow personalities never want you to feel guilty.

What can I do to understand how to recognize the yellow personality quickly?

First, find a "yellow" personality and just listen to that person talk. Notice words in that person's conversations such as:

* Help

* Contribute

* Assist

* Feel

* Nurture

* Comfort

* Care

* Share

Etc.

Just by understanding their natural vocabulary and the words they choose to describe their lives, we can quickly determine their personality color, even over the telephone.

Second, make a list of all the yellow personalities you know. That person at work, your aunt, the minister, the volunteer ... and make the list as big as you possibly can.

By observing the people on your yellow list, you will understand what yellows say, what they do, and you will easily recognize the next yellow stranger you meet, especially if that stranger gives you a cookie.

How to invite a yellow personality to an opportunity meeting.

Here is an **exaggerated** example of how you would talk to a yellow personality in their natural yellow language.

All you are doing is informing them that you want them to come to your opportunity meeting, but you are putting your request in the language they understand. Here is your invitation:

"I want to ask you for a favor. We have an opportunity meeting tomorrow night, would you please come? We need your **help**.

"We market some skin-care products that **help** women look younger, feel better about themselves, and lead happier, more confident lives. And we have some nutritional products that help young mothers have more energy so they can balance their families, their careers, and their personal lives.

"We also give young mothers a chance to work out of their homes, so they can be with their children, and stop warehousing their babies in daycare, paying strangers big money to watch their children grow up. Just think of all the commuting pollution we could reduce by helping people work out of their homes.

"And I just need to bring one more guest to the meeting so that I can win the 'secret ribbon of happiness' award. Would you please come with me to be my guest?

"Oh, and could you bring some refreshments also?"

Yes, your yellow prospect is coming.

The exaggerated script above communicates your invitation in the yellow language, so your yellow prospect wants to come. The yellow person will see what you see, that something good will happen at the meeting.

Remember, the **skill** is to quickly understand if you are talking to a yellow personality.

The words we use when we talk to yellow personalities are easy. And by adding just a few words such as "help" … "care" … etc., we will communicate with the yellows in a way they understand.

Now, you don't have to change who you are. You don't have to change the color personality you are.

All you have to do is translate your normal conversation into the yellow language.

Oh, I want to throw up!

Now, if the previous example of the yellow invitation doesn't resonate with you, makes you ill, or you just don't get it … don't worry.

That only means that you are not a yellow personality. You just see the world differently through one of the other three colors.

So let's take a look at the next color personality now.

The "blue" personality.

The second personality is easy. I can describe the blue personality in one word:

"Party!"

* Blues love to party.

* Blues love to have fun.

* Blues love adventure.

* Blues love trying new things.

* Blues love to travel.

* And most importantly, blues love meeting new people.

Would that be important in network marketing?

Yes!

Blues were made for network marketing, because the blues have never met a stranger. Everyone they meet is instantly their friend. They start a conversation right away.

You already know about the blue personalities because you see them every day.

When you get on the elevator, and a blue personality gets on the elevator with you, the blue starts telling you his life story. He tells you where the family went last night, who they met, what they are going to do today. And you haven't said a word!

The blue personalities are the easiest of all the personalities to recognize ... because they are always **talking**. They talk from the moment they wake up in the morning, all the way through lunch, all the way through the afternoon, all the way through the evening, and they even talk in their sleep! They talk and talk and talk. If there is a gap in the conversation, they fill that gap with words, just to be talking.

If you have a blue leader on your team, they are going to bring lots of new people into your business, lots of people to the meetings, lots of people to the conventions ... yes, the blue personalities are natural promoters.

If a blue personality goes to a movie, from the moment the blue leaves the theater, he is saying, "Oh, what a great movie. You've got to see this movie. Let me tell you about all the best parts of this movie."

And this will be the best movie the blue ever watched until ... the next movie!

Blues were born to be promoters. Network marketing is a perfect fit for the blues.

So if the blue personality is always talking, what would be the downside?

They never **listen**. Now, they are not being rude by not listening to you.

What is happening is that the blue personalities are thinking at 200 miles an hour, in 200 different directions, all at the same time! The other personalities just think too slowly for them.

So they finish our sentences for us, they finish our paragraphs for us, they don't even slow down to listen to us, they just keep on talking.

In my live workshops, I ask the attendees, "Would all the blue personalities please raise their hands?"

No one raises their hand. Why?

Because the blue personalities aren't listening, of course.

I have a friend named Michael. He is blue. When Michael and I go out recruiting together, I drive and Michael talks. He answers his own questions.

But when Michael drives? When he drives, he still does all the talking, but he considers the rules of the road only a suggestion. Blues love adventure.

When Michael calls me at home, I pick up the phone, say hello, put the phone down, go to the kitchen and make a sandwich, watch some television, come back 30 minutes later, and he will still be talking.

Here is Michael's schedule. He starts his telephone day around 9:00 in the morning. He does conference calls, he does trainings, he prospects, and he coaches and mentors and talks and talks and talks until midnight.

However, his wife Linda ... she does all the work, all the follow-up, all the support, sends out the welcome packs, makes sure people remember the next meeting, registers the distributors for training ... because she is a yellow personality. That is what yellows do, they support.

During the day while Michael is talking, she walks by and says, "Do you want a neck rub? Want a sandwich? Need a soda?"

I asked Linda one day, "So Linda, how does it feel to be married to Michael?" (Remember, she is a yellow personality.)

Linda answered, "Oh, it is so wonderful. Michael goes out and meets all these brand-new people and I get to nurture them and support them."

Isn't that a great team? Michael meets lots of new people, and she gets to do all of the follow-up.

She has to. Why? Because the blues will never, ever follow up. Do you know why? Because they are too busy meeting **new** people.

Now, since the blues are out there meeting new people, and thinking at 200 miles an hour, it appears to the rest of us that they have very short attention spans. When you are talking to the blues, they will change the subject of their conversation five or six times before you get a chance to say anything.

For example, if you are conducting a meeting, a blue personality will raise his hand and ask a question because … he just has to talk! The question might sound like this:

"I have a question. I was driving over to Chicago with my new distributor. We were going there to see a prospect, and we were driving over in my Volvo because the Mercedes was broken. I can't believe what they were going to charge me for an alternator on the Mercedes. For that amount of money you could fly to Disney World. It is unbelievable, the cost of foreign car repairs. When I first flew to Disney World, I was in the 4th grade. And down there in Disney World you can pick oranges off the trees. It is totally different from when you get fresh oranges from the grocery store that really aren't that fresh. And of course, our 4th grade teacher, she was a sister-in-law of my mother's first husband. We went down there as part of a group trip, and we had groups join us from Indiana, Illinois and even Wisconsin. It is cold in Wisconsin in the winter, don't really know how they can live there. But I saw a show on television about Canada and how the moose population is dwindling because of global warming ..."

Five minutes later, the blue personality finishes the question. You ask yourself, "How do I answer that?" And then you realize that you don't have to, because the blue person just wanted to talk. No one would be listening to your answer anyway!

You'll know when you have a blue prospect at your opportunity meeting, because halfway through the meeting, the blue prospect will jump up out of his chair and run outside because he just **has to talk**. The blue prospect will then meet a stranger in the hallway, and instantly he will begin talking and say:

"Oh man, you have to join us. This is going to be terrific. Wow, they have these trips coming up, the travel, we are going to meet lots of new people, fun, wonderful meetings, it is going to be so awesome.

"I can't remember the name of the company, can't remember what it is about, but just join! This will be incredible!"

Yes, that is a true blue personality. They are the "big picture" people. They don't worry about those tiny little details like the name of the company or the products.

The skill is being able to spot the blue personality.

Remember, the secret language of each personality is easy. Just a couple of words. The real skill is being able to recognize the color personality your prospect is … quickly.

Blues are easy to spot because they are always talking. They are full of life. Whenever I see a three-year-old moonwalking at the shopping mall, I say to myself, "Yep, that is a blue personality. And the parents are in for a long, long childhood of trying to get that child to focus."

Let's look at some examples of blue personalities.

Mel Gibson in the movie *Lethal Weapon* was blue. He was a crazy cop, wanting constant action, and you felt like he would say, "Let's go out and shoot some people, fill out the reports later, then ask questions." Action, action, action.

Blues take action, don't need to be bothered with information and facts, and are out building their network marketing business before they even know what the products do. You have to love people with that kind of action mentality.

Blues spend their time in action, and they don't waste their time with pondering and thinking. They are just out there making it happen. If you want something to happen, get the blues on it.

If a blue landed at your local airport, the first thing he would say is, "Oh, what sightseeing tour can we do first? What parties can we go to tonight? What kind of fun can we have now?"

John Cleese, in the British comedy *Fawlty Towers*, was a great example of a blue personality. Constant activity in a hundred different directions simultaneously, with little accomplished, wanting to have fun.

Or how about the English comedian, Benny Hill? Every show was 30 seconds of frantic activity, lots of laughs, lots of fun, and then on to the next 30 seconds of frantic activity, laughs, and more fun.

Cartoon characters?

Bugs Bunny and SpongeBob SquarePants. Definitely characters who love to have fun. Not shy, always wanting something new and interesting.

The Disney character, Goofy, was all about living in the moment, no planning, having fun, and he did that with a 24-hour smile on his face, no matter how much trouble he was in.

Homer Simpson? Definitely blue. Never thought things out, didn't plan, just lived every moment and enjoyed life as best he could. And yes, his wife Marge was the yellow personality who took care of all the messes that Homer made.

In the movie *Finding Nemo*, the fast-talking blue tang fish named Dory had a short memory but was always cheerful and ready for the next adventure. She was ultra-blue.

What about Charlie Brown's dog, Snoopy? Of course Snoopy was a blue. Always having fun, imagining himself as a pilot ... blues live in the present.

On the children's show, *Sesame Street*, can you think of some blue personalities? How about Ernie? Full of fun, mischief, enjoying every moment of every day. Or how about the Cookie Monster? He lived in the moment, was excited every time he saw a cookie, was full of life, and had … blue fur!

Blue behavior.

Remember that banquet?

Imagine that the blue personality enters a large banquet room. There are large round tables, some with many happy, laughing people, and one table where a person sits by himself.

At which table will the blue personality sit?

Well, not at the table with only one lonely person. That is where the yellow personality sat.

Instead, the blue personality will find the loudest table, the most excited table, where there is no room to sit, and the blue personality will pull up a chair and join in that table's fun and conversation. The blue personality wants to meet the maximum number of new people.

Blue personalities just **have** to be around people.

One of my granddaughters is a blue personality. When she was small, she was always dancing, jumping and quick to try new, interesting things. Even when she was two years old, she never wandered off alone. She just naturally wanted to be with other people.

Blues want to be where the action is.

Do blues make great leaders?

Of course! They are action people. They are not going to wait around while some committee makes a decision. They want to be in action now.

Their group doesn't have to worry about what to do on the company holiday. The blues already have the excursions booked and the music is already playing.

Why your prospects don't understand you.

Consider the word, "banquet."

Does the word banquet mean something different to the yellow and blue personalities?

Yes.

To the blues, banquet means a chance to talk, have fun and meet new people.

To the yellows, banquet means a chance to make sure everyone is happy and no one is left out.

And that is the problem in communication. Almost every word in your presentation can mean something completely different, depending on the color language your prospect understands.

If every word you say can mean something different to a different personality, is it now obvious why people don't join our programs or buy our products?

If we speak in a different color language than our prospect understands, there will be confusion and misunderstanding, and that person won't join us or buy from us.

The skill is to recognize the blue personality quickly.

Thankfully, that isn't hard.

If you find yourself standing around while the other person talks and talks, well, you have found a blue personality. So notice the words in that person's conversations, such as:

* Fun

* Excellent

* Awesome

* Interesting

* Travel

* New

* Exciting

And then notice how they are **not listening to you**!

You might hear these words in a conversation that goes something like this:

"My job isn't **fun** anymore. It is the same old thing day after day. Boring. I am looking for something where I can go out and meet **new, interesting** people and not be **stuck** behind a desk."

How to invite a blue personality
to an opportunity meeting.

Here is an **exaggerated** example of how you would talk to a blue personality in their natural blue language.

Again, all you are doing is informing them that you want them to come to your opportunity meeting, but you are putting your request in the language they understand. Here is your invitation:

First, wait for the blue personality to take a breath, and a sip out of his soda. This is your chance to say something really quickly before he starts talking again. Here is your invitation:

"We have a meeting tomorrow night. It is going to be so exciting, so much fun. You will have a chance to meet lots of new people and get to talk to them before the meeting, during the meeting, and for hours after the meeting. We have free trips we can win to Las Vegas and to London, and we take a 747 airplane, put a barrel of iced beer in the aisle, sing karaoke and have a big party on the way to our holiday. And once we get to the holiday, we take tours all day long, party all night, stay awake for 96 straight hours … and you've just got to come, I need a roommate for the trip …"

Hey, the blue personality is ready to join now and start talking to people. The blue personality doesn't even need a presentation! This sounds like too much fun, so the decision to join has already been made.

What is really great about talking to blues is that they aren't really listening. So if you forget what to say, just say anything really fast and with excitement. It works.

The "red" personality.

The third personality is the "red" personality, and these people:

* Want to be in charge.

* Want to be the boss.

* Want to tell other people what to do.

* Are great organizers.

* Are bottom-line people who want results.

* Hate people with whiny excuses.

* And are all about the … **money**!

The red personalities earn the most money in network marketing. Sure, the blues will talk to more people, but the reds organize their teams and demand results.

Everyone would love a red leader on their team. Why? They would do it their way and get the job done, with no input or requests from you.

If you didn't have red leaders on your team, who would organize the meetings? Not the yellows. They would say, "Oh, let's have a meeting, sit in a semi-circle, sing the company song, and eat cookies. Then we can discuss what we should do at the meeting. Maybe we should let someone else organize the meeting and be in charge, and we will help them and support them."

And the blues? Hey, the blues can't organize two thoughts in a row without changing the subject. You don't want your blue leaders organizing anything!

That is why the red personalities are so important. They take charge and get things done.

You will find red personalities as bosses, managers, and politicians. Yes, politicians are red. They say, "Elect me and then I will tell you what to do."

You need the reds to organize things. For example, if you needed a wedding planner, would you want a yellow personality as your wedding planner? She might say, "Oh yes, my cat was sick, so I didn't talk to the baker and that is why your cake is yellow instead of white. The poor baker, she lost her dog a few weeks ago, and hasn't felt the same since."

No, you want a red wedding planner who makes sure your wedding goes without a hitch, with perfect military efficiency.

Some examples of the red personality.

Margaret Thatcher of England was red. Confronting people was her style. She wanted things her way.

Donald Trump is red. He is all about the money. He doesn't hesitate to say, "You're fired!" if someone doesn't meet his expectations.

Top athletes and people with huge egos are red personalities. They have to be #1 at everything.

Mr. Burns, the greedy nuclear plant owner in *The Simpsons* is totally red. And so is the beast in *Beauty and the Beast*.

In the British comedy *Fawlty Towers*, the domineering wife Sybil was red. She didn't listen to any nonsense, and insisted things get done. She had to be red because her husband, John Cleese, was completely blue and needed strong guidance.

From the really old television shows, Archie Bunker and George Jefferson were reds that never listened, and always felt they had the right answers to everything.

And Lucy, from the cartoon strip *Peanuts*? She wanted to be the boss and tell Charlie Brown and the others what to do. Always willing to give her opinion and dispense advice, Lucy was thoroughly red.

Reds don't listen either!

The yellows are all about helping people, the blues are all about having fun (yes, the blues will have the most fun in network marketing) and the reds are all about the money. But the reds won't listen.

Now, reds won't listen because they already have all the right answers. Why would they listen to our puny little wrong opinions when they already know everything? Reds have never been wrong ... about anything!

That means if you have red leaders on your team, they are not listening to you. They already know how they are going to do their business, how they are going to run their campaigns, and how they are going to build their groups. You know you have a red leader in your upline when the red leader says this:

"Okay team, let's get together. We are all buying 500 leads. I want a list of 200 names of your hottest prospects on my desk by tomorrow morning. Plus, I also want everybody here to make 50 cold calls every day, knock on 33 doors, and have two guests at every opportunity meeting. It is my way or the highway."

Reds love competition and recognition.

The reds will make the most money because they are very competitive. They love competition. If there is a trophy, the reds want the recognition of winning the trophy. They see every trophy as a place to showcase their name.

If a red personality came in 4th place in a competition, the red personality would call up the people who placed 5th, 6th, 7th, 8th, 9th, and 10th in the competition and say, "Hey, loser! Look where I am!"

Yes, reds love winning.

Would you like to see how a red gets a trophy?

When a red gets a trophy at the big meeting, he says, "Thank you for the trophy. I worked hard for this, I deserve this, and you are all losers!"

Would you like to see how a yellow personality gets that same trophy?

The yellow personality receives the trophy and says, "Boo hoo hoo. Sniffle. Cry, cry, cry. I don't really deserve this trophy. We should give the trophy to poor Mary, she has a sick cat at home, and this trophy could cheer her up."

Would you like to see how a blue personality gets that same trophy? He receives the trophy and instantly starts talking at 200 miles an hour saying, "Trophy! This reminds me of my trip to Disney World. We had little umbrellas in our drinks on the way down on the plane. Do you know who I sat next to? She shopped for shoes at the same place my aunt shops for shoes. It is next to the new mall they are going to build. It will have an awesome bowling alley. Can't wait to play in a league there …"

Wow. The simple act of receiving a trophy could have three different meanings, depending on which personality you are talking to.

Is it getting easier to understand that what we say could mean one thing to us, but could mean something completely different to a different color personality?

You need everyone.

Yes, you need reds on your team to organize and keep everyone focused. You need blues on your team to bring in lots of new people. Plus the blues will make your meetings more fun and exciting. They are better known as "boredom busters!"

And of course we need the yellows to support and help at all our events, and to make peace and keep everyone happy.

All three colors make great leaders.

Red behavior.

Remember that banquet? What happens when a red personality goes to that banquet?

Well, the red walks into the banquet room, immediately takes charge, grabs the microphone, rearranges the tables, tells everyone where to sit, and announces the agenda for the evening.

Reds were made to be in charge and to organize everything. And that is important.

Do you remember those 12 yellow personalities having a meeting? Remember how they were going to starve because no one was willing to suggest a place to eat for fear of offending someone?

If a red personality walked into that meeting, the red personality would say, "We are all going to eat at the cafeteria on the first floor. The service is quick, and we can all be back to work here in 20 minutes. Leave now and don't be late coming back!"

The 12 yellow personalities would all cheer and be excited that they get a chance to eat, and they didn't have to personally make the final decision.

Red personalities are red.

When you talk to a red personality, you will notice that the red personalities often think they are ... yellow! Just ask them their color and they will reply, "Oh, I am yellow. I am just helping these poor losers by telling them what to do. These idiots can't even take care of themselves, so I am reorganizing them so they can get something done."

Yeah, these reds **think** they are yellow, but we know better.

The skill is to recognize the red personality quickly.

Thankfully, again, this isn't hard.

If you find yourself swallowing hard while the other person tells you "how it is" ... you are probably talking to a red. Listen for words such as:

* Money

* Power

* Wealth

* Compete

* Losers

* Whiners

* Results

* Control

* Boss

* Leader

* Image

And if you are talking to a prospect, and the prospect says,

"Stop the chit-chat. Get to the point. How many people do I have to sponsor to make $1,000?"

That's a clue. That person is a red personality.

Remember to look for these traits.

* They are "bottom-line" people. They want you to get to the facts, especially the facts about money.

* They are "all about the money" – they use money to measure their success in business. So when you say "big money" ... you are speaking their language.

* They are great organizers, and that's why you need reds on your team. Who else would organize the meetings and the trainings?

* They like to be the boss. They are at their best when they are in charge. Reds make lousy followers. They love telling other people what to do.

Stay out of their way.

The reds will have their own system, their own team, their own campaigns … and your job is to stay out of their way and support them any way you can.

They are going to do it "their way" because they know exactly how they want their business to be duplicated. They are not looking to take orders or suggestions from you.

And your reward for staying out of their way?

Well, first, they will take care of the problems in their group. They won't be passing problems up to you.

And second, they will earn you a lot of money. So sit back and enjoy.

How to invite a red personality to an opportunity meeting.

Here is an **exaggerated** example of how you would talk to a red personality in their natural red language.

Again, all you are doing is informing them that you want them to come to your opportunity meeting, but you are putting your request in the language they understand.

"We have an opportunity meeting tomorrow night. Be there. We are talking money. Lots of money. Huge amounts

44

of money. Not that little money from having a job, but the big money from having your own business.

"Here is your chance to fire the boss, be your own boss, have your own organization, and tell them what to do. You can be #1 in the state and get the recognition you deserve. Plus, you can finally get a bonus check that recognizes your greatness, then buy that red Ferrari that you've always wanted, drive back to where you used to work, leave rubber marks up and down the company parking lot, roll down the window and wave saying, 'Good-bye losers!'"

Only reds understand these sentences. To them, when you say these sentences, it is like you're reading their minds. They are in agreement, nothing more to discuss. They will be at your opportunity meeting early, sitting in the front row.

Now, if you are not a red personality, you won't understand these sentences. You don't get it. In fact, if you are a yellow personality you are thinking, "Oh, that is so cruel."

But this is the language of the red personality.

The "green" personality.

The green personalities are your:

* Engineers

* Accountants

* Computer geeks

* Scientists

Yes, green personalities are boring people, personality-free, charisma-bypassed, and should not be let out in public.

While the yellows are all about **helping** people, the blues are all about having **fun**, and the reds are all about the **money** ... the greens are only interested in:

Information!

The word "data" actually gets the greens excited.

Now, while the other color personalities have good points and bad points, the green personalities only have good points. Oh, by the way, did I mention that I am a green personality?

For the greens, our poster boy is Mr. Spock from *Star Trek*. Remember him? All about logic, all about the facts, all about information, and no emotion.

In the comic strip *Dilbert*, both Dilbert and his friend Wally are green. They are both slightly fashion-impaired and see the world in black and white, with no shades of gray. Wally and Dilbert's views of the world are logic, data, and then more information.

Sesame Street? How about Count von Count as he focused on the details of counting everything? And you have to admit that Ernie's friend, Bert, was a bit of an anti-social green personality.

You know you are talking to a green prospect when you finish your three-hour presentation and the green prospect says, "Thank you for your **preliminary** information. I will now go on the Internet and research 44 different websites, set up an Excel spreadsheet and a database, make them relational, interactive ... and I will get back to you in about 3.7 weeks."

So if you are looking for a quick decision from a green personality, you will only be frustrated. Greens drive the red and blue personalities crazy as they delay decisions and activity. Their motivation is collecting all the information available, and then pondering all the possibilities and potential future scenarios to make sure no mistake is made.

Green personalities are very comfortable with books and computers, and very uncomfortable around humans.

So the green personalities you encounter will spend far too much time thinking and far too little time acting. Just the opposite of the blue personality that spends far too much time acting, and too little time thinking. My blue friend, Michael, says,

"My life would be so much better if it wasn't for those green personalities. I call them up, and I say, 'Hey! You have been a distributor for six months already. Just talk to someone!' And the green personalities will answer, 'Well, there are two more questions I have to translate into Swahili, just in case the first person I meet only understands Swahili. I want to be prepared before I start.'"

Why do green personalities have to accumulate all this information? Of course they want to be sure to make the right decision, but they also want to be able to answer any questions for their downline.

What is great about the green personalities is that once they make their decision, they stay with it. They went through all the effort, all the facts, they weighed all the possible options, so once they have made their decision, they are going to stay with it for a long, long time. Greens may not be very fast starters, but they will be the people that stick with you for the long haul.

This means that green personalities make great leaders also.

When someone in their downline calls up with a question, the green personality knows the answer. And if you need to know the answer to a compensation plan question or about a magic ingredient, they have the answer for that too.

Greens spend all their time preparing for this, so if a downline distributor calls up and asks for an application form from 1982, they will reply, "Do you want Revision A or Revision B? I have both in inventory."

Green personalities spend all their time going to trainings, re-writing brochures, accumulating information ... because these activities help them avoid talking to people. Network marketing, talking to people, is a bit out of the comfort zone of most green personalities. They have to be fully prepared before they will have the confidence to talk to their first prospect.

On the plus side, green personalities are extremely loyal. They have already investigated all competing companies, and have chosen their current company as the best.

Green behavior.

If the yellows are the professional huggers, the greens would be the anti-huggers. Greens just aren't good around people. If you try to hug a green personality, they turn into an icicle and try to slip away.

My blue friend, Michael, likes to tease me because I am green. Sometimes I go to Canada to visit my green friend, Gary. Michael will call up Gary and say, "Hey Gary, when Big Al comes to visit you, I want you to give him a big hug! And please take a picture of this because two greens hugging has never been seen before!"

So if the greens are the anti-huggers, the yellows are professional huggers, then what about the blues? How do the blues feel about hugging? They would say, "Woo-hoo! Sounds like fun!"

And what about the reds? If you asked a red personality to hug, he might say, "How much bonus money would I get for that?"

The simple event of hugging can mean up to four different things, which means almost every word in your presentation can mean up to four different things depending on the color language that the prospect understands.

It should be crystal clear now why people don't buy or join. They just don't understand us because they are interpreting our words differently, because they speak a different language.

More green behavior.

You know you are married to a green when the green plans a family vacation. The green personality knows how many miles between every fuel station, and which station has the lowest price (pre-checked on the Internet.) He booked the hotels nine months in advance to get the lowest possible price, and there is a schedule for everything that must be followed.

If a doorknob falls off in your house, the green personality will spend three months investigating why it fell off and then write a prevention manual for loose doorknobs. Then the green personality will spend six months shopping locally for the best possible replacement value, then compare those prices with Internet prices around the world. When the replacement doorknob arrives, it is delivered with $250 worth of power tools and $300 worth of installation manuals. Ah, but when that doorknob gets replaced, it will be the best doorknob you have ever seen.

During one of my workshops, a green personality gave me his business card during the break. Okay, it really wasn't a business card. It was actually paper that was cut in the shape of a business card because that was cheaper. On his business card, he had written his entire one-minute business presentation, front and back, in tiny print that you could barely read.

I looked at his business card and said, "What's this?"

He answered, "Well, it is my business card. What do you think of it? And I have a plan. At night, when everyone in the neighborhood is asleep, I will sneak out and put these business cards underneath their windshield wipers on their cars. When my neighbors wake up in the morning, they will read my one-minute presentation on this business card and then they will join my business. I won't even have to talk to them!"

Well, maybe disaster is awaiting this plan. However, there could be another green personality in his neighborhood and this could happen:

That green neighbor walks out to his car in the morning and says, "Hmm, there appears to be a piece of paper, roughly the dimensions of a business card, underneath my windshield wiper. I wonder what it says. Let me pull out my handy magnifying glass from my toolkit and read the micro-print. Hmm, this appears to be an interesting offer. Let me go on the Internet and see if I can sign up on my own. Maybe I could give myself a cool I.D. number such as 007."

Okay, I did say it **could** happen, but probably not. This is just how greens think. Green personalities will do almost anything to avoid contact with new prospects.

What would greens do at banquets?

Ha, ha, ha. Trick question. Greens don't go to banquets because there are people at the banquets. The green personality stays home and surfs the Internet instead.

Greens marry spouses of a different color personality and send them to the banquet.

Yes, the word banquet means something else entirely to the greens.

You are probably wondering, "How does a green get a trophy?"

Well, remember how the yellow got the trophy? "Somebody else deserves it more."

And the blue got the trophy and started talking endlessly about whatever came to mind.

The red said, "I am a winner and you are all losers."

But what about the greens?

Well, we don't get trophies. We are too busy reading the rules and checking for typos in the announcement. We never get started in time.

Again, trophies mean something completely different to the greens.

How do green personalities handle pain?

Imagine a green personality goes to his little workshop in the basement of his home. Accidentally, the green hits his fingers with his hammer. The pain instantly shoots up his arm and alarms go off in his brain.

What does the green do? He asks himself, "I wonder if the pain in my fingers has anything to do with the impact of the hammer crushing those bones. I should be sure."

So again, the green hits his fingers with his hammer. And again, intense pain is felt and alarms go off.

The green thinks, "Yes, there seems to be a relationship between the pain in my fingers and the impact of hammers. I believe I have proven this relationship exists. Let me do it one more time to prove my new theory, just to be sure."

Green personalities are skeptical. They need proof. They want to be sure before they make their decisions.

So expect delays in decisions and actions from green personalities. And then, once they are sure, you can expect focus and loyalty. That's the payoff.

Green fashion.

Oh, those words should never go together.

Of all the color personalities, greens are the most challenged when it comes to fashion. Why?

Because there is no manual with checklists for fashion. I am still searching for the manual with all those fashion rules made up by an unseen committee.

Fashion is more of an art than a science, and to us green personalities, if there are no hard and fast rules, then we are going to be … clueless.

Who was the person who made the rule that striped shirts shouldn't be worn with khaki shorts and black socks? Why shouldn't a thin-striped red power tie be worn with a paisley shirt?

Why green engineers don't dance.

Have you ever seen a green engineer dance? It is very mechanical. Would you like to know what goes through his head while dancing?

"Engage process #1: lift right foot 5.5 centimeters, shift weight 62% to the left foot, make a 90 degree arc with the right foot, turn 180 degrees, repeat process #1 with the left foot …"

We need green personalities.

Lots of people make fun of the greens because they struggle to get started in network marketing with poor people skills, but remember this. When you are crossing a bridge, you'd better hope it was built by a green. You don't want that bridge built by a blue. If the blue was in charge of building that bridge, the conversation during construction might go something like this:

"Oh, it's not level over there. Put another beer can under it."

Green personalities make great security guards. Could you imagine a yellow personality as a security guard? When the yellow sees the criminal stealing the company computers, the yellow might say, "Oh, those are really heavy. Do you need some help? Please tell me about the trauma of your youth."

So we need the greens, we need the yellows, we need the blues, and yes, we need the reds. All have a part in making our organizations grow.

**How to invite a green personality
to an opportunity meeting.**

Again, here is an **exaggerated** example of how you would talk to a green personality in their natural green language.

"Would you please come to the meeting tomorrow night? I need your **opinion**. We are going to sit way in the back of the room, where nobody will bother us, nobody will ask us to join ... and bring a huge notebook, because there will be lots of information. And hopefully, by the end of the meeting, we will have enough information to begin our preliminary research."

Ka-ching!

We green personalities are there. We feel comfortable, because that is our language.

The green personalities, like the yellow personalities, don't like to be sold. This invitation is perfect for the green prospects in your life.

And if we used that same green invitation, but said it to a blue personality … well, that blue prospect would have finished a six-pack of beer and left for more excitement before we finished the invitation.

So what color personality are you?

Some people are so blue you just know their personality color right away. Whenever I see a four-year-old boy breakdancing and singing at the airport, I know his parents are going to have a long and interesting journey raising this blue boy.

Some people are so red that it is easy to classify their color. When I see a young girl bossing around her peers and commanding the playground, I see a future politician or manager. She was born to lead and rule.

I love it when people are easy to recognize. Then you don't need a huge personality test or questionnaire because you just know right away what color they are.

But what about you?

What color personality do you think you are?

Most people have one primary color, and maybe a bit of another color. For myself, I am 100% green so I don't have to stress wondering what color I am. (Yes, I researched all the alternatives before deciding that I am 100% green.)

If you are unsure of your personality color, here are some reasons that it may not be clear to you.

Reason #1: You are a yellow personality and are thinking, "Oh, I wish somebody could come and tell me what color I am."

Reason #2: You are a blue personality and you only skimmed this book so far and you really weren't paying attention.

Reason #3: You are a green personality and you are thinking, "I need a lot more information before I make my final decision."

Okay, just kidding about those reasons. Actually, the reds always know what color they are. If you ask them their own color personality, they reply, "We are red. We are the best color, and we don't need those other stupid colors."

What if I feel that I am all the colors?

We call that "psychotic."

Multiple personality disorder. :)

Okay, we all have a little bit of all the colors, but usually one color stands out the most, and maybe we have a secondary color that is pretty prominent also.

You'll hear people say, "Oh, I am blue, but I also have some yellow." Yes, it is okay for blue personalities to care about people. It is okay for a green to occasionally speak up and take charge of a meeting.

And if you feel you are two colors, that simply means that you can speak two of the color languages natively.

That's great, and you should congratulate yourself. You only have to learn the other two languages, and then you will be able to communicate with everyone in their own native language.

Ask your friends.

We don't see ourselves from an unbiased viewpoint. So if you are not sure what color personality you are, simply ask your friends!

They will be glad to tell you the color personality you are. To them it is obvious.

My job color ... or is it my personal color?

Many people do not know what color personality they are because they confuse their personal color with their job color.

It is your **personal** color that is important. Jobs can come and go, but you will remain the same color personality.

Concentrate on what color you feel you are, and don't let your current job influence your judgment. Here's why.

Let's say that Anna is yellow. She loves hugging people. One day she gets hired in a customer service department, helping other people. Anna is so good at helping people at her job, she gets promoted to ... manager! Ooops. Red personalities love to be managers, but yellow personalities hate being managers. Now Anna hates her job because now she has to fire people.

Anna is still a yellow personality, but she is now working in a red job, as a manager that has to fire people. Poor Anna. She cries every night. She is a yellow trapped in a red job, and she hates her life.

A lot of job dissatisfaction comes from people who have chosen a career that doesn't match their color personality.

So forget the job. Look deep inside your prospects to find their true color personalities.

Want another example?

Imagine a blue personality stuck in a job as an accountant! That person is still a blue personality, but just stuck in a green job. Actually, it would be funny just to watch that blue personality in the accounting job. I could see him saying, "Hey, the numbers don't add up! Let's have another beer!"

I don't think I want my accountant to be a blue personality.

We all speak the color language of our primary color easily.

That is why it is easy for accountants to talk to other accountants, and for managers to talk to managers, and for two blue personalities to talk at the same time, and both are happy!

Some people are like me, all one color. I like being 100% green.

And some people just don't see themselves realistically. I had one lady tell me, "Oh, I am orange - that is, I am yellow with red ascending on the horizon."

No, no, no. No orange, no red, just an out-of-touch yellow personality who thinks about her feelings too much.

So, I told this lady, "You are yellow! So get on your imaginary unicorn and ride out and meet the world."

She replied, "Okay, I will be a yellow then. I mean, if it is okay with you." :)

You have to love the yellow personalities.

You still have to do tasks each day that are associated with the other color personalities.

If you are a fun-loving blue personality, you still have to balance a check book and pay your taxes. And showing up for work on time may be a challenge, but it is something you have to try to do after a hard night of having fun.

If you are a kind, yellow personality, you still have to take charge and get the kids ready for the school or insist that your dental patient take good care of his teeth.

If you are a red personality, and your three-year-old daughter comes to you with a splinter in her finger, you have to be yellow for at least a little while.

Most husbands say this: "My wife is so red. She always tells me what to do." But if the wife won't train her husband, then who will?

If you are a green personality, you still have to move 13 muscles on each side of your mouth to form a smile when you are forced to be at social functions.

"I am still not sure what color I am."

Let's make this even easier. Which are the two **outgoing** color personalities?

The blue and the red.

Imagine that a red upline leader promotes a sponsoring campaign. She says, "I want everyone on the team to talk to 50 strangers this week!"

Well, the outgoing red distributors on the team will be thinking, "I can talk to my 50 strangers before the rest of the team even gets started."

The outgoing blue distributors on the team will be thinking, "All right! We get to talk to strangers! This will be fun. Awesome. Let's go meet some strangers now."

But the yellows and the greens? They are quieter, not nearly so outgoing. They do their sponsoring differently. They are not comfortable accosting total strangers. Instead, they will talk to fewer people, get to know them and build a relationship, and then introduce their business.

Of course the reds think the greens and yellows are a bunch of whiny losers because they are not talking to every stranger they meet. The reds don't understand that their way is not the only way to build a business.

Okay, so understanding which personalities are outgoing helps.

If you are outgoing, there is a pretty good chance that you might be a blue or a red, right? But how do you know if you, as an outgoing person, are a blue or a red?

Well, if you are already talking ... you are probably a blue.

And if you are a red personality, then you are already thinking, "I don't need any of those other three stupid, useless colors." :)

What about the quieter colors?

If you are quieter, you are probably yellow or green. But, which one?

Well, there are two quick tests you can give yourself.

Test #1: Ask yourself, "Do I have a personality?"

If the answer is yes, you are a yellow.

Test #2: Ask someone to give you a huge hug and see what happens. :)

This movie example tells it all.

Jerry "D'Rhino" Clark gave me this story about the color personalities. In the movie *Titanic*, the ship hits an iceberg and sinks. So what are the different personalities doing while the ship sinks?

1. The yellows are fluffing the pillows in the lifeboats so the survivors will feel comfortable.

2. The blues are still at the bar with the band. Why not? The drinks are now free.

3. The reds have already organized and left in the first lifeboats available.

4. The greens are calculating the pressure in pounds per square inch that would have been necessary for the iceberg to penetrate the hull.

Bottom line: It doesn't really matter what color you are.

All of the colors are good. You are born with your color personality, so relax, enjoy your color and don't stress yourself by trying to change your color.

What **does** matter is the color your prospects are.

You want to talk to your prospects with language that is familiar and comfortable to them. We want our message to go straight to their minds and to their hearts, with no translation needed on their part.

Discovering your prospect's secret language.

Remember, the real skill here is figuring out **quickly** what color personality your prospect is. Once you know your prospect's color, just a few words in your prospect's language is all you need to communicate clearly.

The easiest way to learn that skill is to actually do it. So are you ready to try this out in real life?

I want you to pick a partner now. Maybe someone in your downline, your spouse, a stranger ... anyone.

Find someone near you now, or maybe pick up the telephone and call someone you know.

Next, I want you to have a little conversation with your partner. Just a short two- or three-minute conversation will do. You and your partner can talk about anything you want. You could discuss the weather, sports, the latest soap opera ... anything that is interesting for both of you to talk about.

At the end of your conversation, ask yourself, "So what color personality was my partner?"

Clear?

Unsure of your partner's color personality?

Before you panic, let me tell you my results.

I can only figure out the color of my prospect about 50% of the time. Half the time, I have absolutely no idea what color my prospect is. Why?

Maybe my prospect is a little bit of everything. Or, maybe I am not paying close attention. I don't know, but I am simply happy picking out the most **obvious** personality colors.

That means that 50% of the time, I have no idea what color personality my prospect is, but I do know that since my prospect is not an extreme version of any of the color personalities, a regular generic presentation will be okay.

But, here is the magic.

The 50% of the time when I **do** know what color my prospect is, all I need to do is say just four or five sentences, and my prospect is ready to buy or join **immediately**. The communication is so clear, so targeted, that when you speak in someone's native color language, they "get it" right away.

I am thrilled with this sort of super-communication with half of the prospects I talk to. You can earn a fortune by super-communicating with half of your prospects. And the great news is that anyone can do this. All you have to do is take advantage of the obvious prospects who have a clear and easy-to-read personality color.

So I hope you feel relieved. You can pick out 50% right now. And if you decide to get better and more observant, great. That just gives you more people you can super-communicate with.

So, are you ready for that test with your partner?

I know what you are thinking:

"Before I talk to my partner, what clues do I look for?"

Would you like some tips?

If your partner says, "Oh, before we talk, would you like some cookies?" Yes, that would be a ... yellow personality.

If the person you chose for your partner is already talking before you even say your first word ... okay, that person would be a blue personality.

If your partner says, "Just get to the point, we don't have a lot of time to waste," then whoa, you're talking to a red personality.

And finally, let's say your partner avoids the conversation and says, "Couldn't we just text or email this instead?" Yes, you would have a green personality as your partner.

Okay, a bit simplistic and exaggerated, but this really is pretty easy.

Have fun practicing!

No agenda means quality conversations.

In the last chapter, you had a chance to call or talk to a friend, and listen carefully for clues to determine that person's color personality.

Now, let's see what happened.

#1. No rejection.

Yes, because your partner was doing most of the talking, there was no chance of you saying something to get rejected. You weren't trying to sneak in a sales pitch at every opportunity. You have heard those "agenda" conversations before. They sound like:

Stranger: "Yeah, my name is William."

Distributor: "William? That is awesome. William starts with the letter "W" just like my current company, World Wide Widgets, and as you know, we make the best widgets known to mankind. Our research scientist can beat up your research scientist. I have testimonial letters from over 80 customers. Let me read them to you now …"

#2. New best friend.

People love great listeners. They sense you are interested in them, and are listening closely to what they say. Because your focus was entirely on your partner in this exercise, you avoided a common error of conversation, which is:

Not listening to the other person because you are too busy trying to figure out what you want to say next. People sense your sincere desire to hear what they have to say.

#3. Easy to do.

Because this simple exercise is easy to do, we won't be fearful when we talk to strangers. Now it is easy to have stress-free conversations wherever we go.

Try this. Let's say that you make a goal of talking to one new person every day. No agenda. No sales pitch. Just talk to one new person every day, and for fun, see if you can pick out that person's color personality. This exercise would only take a minute or two to do every day.

Now, what would happen if you did this?

First, you would get pretty good at recognizing the color personalities of people. It would be fun and entertaining for you.

Second, you would have 365 new contacts who think you are a great listener. What a terrific way to build your warm market of future prospects.

Third, and this is really exciting. Because you were such a good listener, and because you were a **sincere** listener ... 20, 30 or even 40 of these strangers might ask you what you do for a living, or at least want to know more about you. You could have five or ten people literally volunteer to buy what you sell or join your business, just because they like you!

This is truly sponsoring with no rejection.

Now the world makes more sense.

Once we know the four personalities, we can understand why some people act differently than we expect. Here are some great examples.

Blues should not explain anything.

I was introduced to the four different personalities by my friend, Jerry "D'Rhino" Clark. Jerry, of course, is a red personality, but he has a lot of blue personality too. And blue personalities should not explain anything!

Jerry sent me his audio album on the personalities. He had one audio explaining each of the **four** color personalities ... but there were six audios in total. Six???

Yes, it took Jerry two audios to warm up before he got to the point. That's a blue personality explaining things. And when Jerry finally got around to explaining each personality, I just didn't "get it." I couldn't relate to the quadrants, the explanations, and I wasn't really sure how to take the theory and apply it.

Why didn't I understand? Because I am a green personality. We want facts, steps, detailed explanations, and complete instructions on how to put this information into use in real life.

So what happened? I passed on the six audios to a friend of mine, Michael Dlouhy, who is also a blue personality. He "got it" immediately!

Michael put the theory and information to use and had spectacular results. Now, I was really intrigued.

It seems like blue personalities communicate perfectly with each other, but it all sounds like disjointed gibberish to us green personalities.

It was after seeing Michael's results of understanding the four personalities - and after Michael's insistence - that I took on the task to explain this to others in a logical, step-by-step, green manner.

Greens are great at taking complicated ideas and explaining them in a simple way for others to understand.

Blues should be doing things. Blues were made for action.

But greens should explain things. And greens have plenty of time to do this since they have lots of planning to do before they take their first action step.

We are born with a color personality.

Think about it. A couple has four children. From an early age, maybe the oldest child, a girl, has taken on the responsibility of caring for her younger siblings. Her yellow personality and caring just came naturally.

One of her brothers seems undisciplined and has a short attention span. His frantic energy, his need for interaction and constant movement means his parents are going to have years of frustration if they don't realize he is a blue personality. He dances during class at school, wants to explore everything, and sitting still at dinner without singing is impossible.

Another brother appears just the opposite. His green personality helps him focus on reading books, organizing his room, and creating structure and order in his life.

And finally, the younger sister stands on a chair in preschool and gives orders to the other children. Her red personality challenges every request from her parents. She wants to do everything herself and everything turns into a competition.

We marry people of a different color personality.

Why?

Because they have skills and abilities that complement our weaknesses.

For example, what if a green married a blue?

The green could balance the checkbook, make sure things got done on time, and schedule the week. And the green could have fun just watching the blue spouse have fun.

The blue spouse could take care of all the social relationships, entertain their friends, and put a little excitement into their lives.

Or what would happen if a red married a yellow?

The yellow would tolerate the abruptness of the red and understand that maybe the red wasn't being unkind, but was just being direct and to the point.

The red spouse could be in charge of disputing the restaurant bill, something the yellow spouse would never do.

What would happen if someone married a person of the same color personality?

Well, if two yellows got married, they would become missionaries in a foreign country, and you would never see them again.

If two blues got married, that would be a 24-hour hangover, and they would be the loudest neighbors you ever had.

If two reds got married, that would be … war. But who knows, they may form an alliance and then conquer the world.

If two greens got married, well, why bother? It would be more fiscally responsible for them to file their taxes as single individuals.

Why prospects say "No" to great things.

In the beginning of this book, I wrote:

***

Does this look familiar?

Have you ever talked to a prospect and had this happen?

1. The prospect desperately needed your product. (And you just happened to offer this product to your prospect.)

2. The prospect desperately wanted your opportunity. (And you just happened to offer your business to your prospect.)

Then, at the end of your presentation, the prospect says, "No."

What happened?

What went wrong?

Does this seem strange to you?

***

Well, now it probably doesn't look so strange after all.

In fact, it is obvious. We simply talked to our prospect in the wrong color language, and our prospect didn't understand us. Here are some examples of how this misunderstanding shows up in our presentations.

Green vs. Blue.

Imagine a green giving a presentation to a blue. As the green slowly recreates the history of the company, reads the policies and procedures, references the research and awards, and begins the compensation plan explanation … what is the blue doing?

The blue has finished a six-pack of beer and is contemplating jumping off a cliff to avoid any further torture from this green information maniac.

The company could be awesome, but the communication of the company's awesomeness stopped after 30 seconds of mind-numbing facts from the green. The blue will never join, and the blue's decision not to join had nothing to do with how awesome the company was.

Blue vs. Green.

But what happens when a blue gives a presentation to the green? It sounds something like this to the green.

"Let me tell you about the company. I went to my first presentation right after the big game between the Rangers and the Rovers. You should have seen that game. And the hot dogs were awesome. I don't know what they put in those hot dogs, but they are the best hot dogs I have ever eaten except for the time I flew to Germany for Oktoberfest. You wouldn't believe how long that flight is. I think I had five or six of those great drinks where they put those little umbrellas in them. Sort of reminds me of my second cousin's mother who was our teacher in fourth grade. She always threatened us with her English umbrella. Of course we were afraid, those English umbrellas are high-quality and you know they could be lethal. By the way, did you see the movie *Lethal Weapon* with Mel Gibson? Wow. He was all action …"

Will the green ever join? Of course not. Even though the company would be a perfect fit for the green prospect, the green needed all the information to make that decision. And with a blue presentation, no information is ever delivered.

Yellow vs. Red.

Imagine a yellow giving a caring, socially-responsible invitation to an opportunity meeting to a red personality.

"Oh, would you please come to our meeting? Well, it is not really a meeting, as we all sit in a semi-circle, so we all feel equal. And after the company song, we have the cookie-giving ceremony, then there is the group hug …"

Arrrgggghhh! What is the red personality thinking?

"These yellow people are using up valuable oxygen here on earth! They better create more oxygen from their organic gardening. They should pull their own weight and stop being parasites in our business society."

Of course, the red will never join because the red won't even attend the presentation. Hmmm, this might be why yellows don't recruit very many red personalities.

Red vs. Yellow.

Oh, this could get ugly. Here is the short version. The red says this to the yellow:

"Give me all your money, and then I will tell you what it is!"

The yellow doesn't want the red to feel bad or rejected, gives his credit card, goes home, and is afraid of answering his telephone for months because it might be his sponsor.

So that is why people don't join.

We don't need better PowerPoint presentations, and we don't need better videos and brochures. Those things aren't the problem.

The problem is us.

If we fail to translate our message into the color language of our prospect, then nothing will save us.

Three magic questions.

Some prospects are easy. They are so much of their color personality that their color simply shouts out at you.

However, with other prospects, it may not be so easy. They seem a bit reserved; so are they yellow or green? Or they seem more about results and the bottom line; so are they red or green?

I have three magic questions that help guide me in quickly identifying their color personality.

#1. What do you do for a living?

What if your prospect answers, "I am a caseworker for child care services, helping suffering children find better homes." It is a pretty good clue that your prospect is a yellow personality based upon his profession.

Or what if your prospect answered, "I am a computer systems analyst that specializes in integrating machine language code into modern programming languages." Hmmm, there is a good chance this prospect is a green personality based upon his profession.

But this is only a guideline, a hint to look deeper. Why?

Because people may be in a job or profession that doesn't match their true inner personality.

For example, Mary is a yellow personality and she gets a job as a counselor for college admissions. She loves her job and helps students find the right courses and direction in their lives. She is so good at her job, she gets promoted to be the manager of all the counselors. Now she spends every day monitoring reports and paperwork, and sometimes she has to fire people! She now hates her job.

This often happens when people choose a job closer to where they live that doesn't match their personality.

Here is another common scenario. A child is a blue personality, but is forced to become an accountant by his parents who were accountants. Every day is then torture.

So finding out what people do for a living isn't foolproof. But it does serve as a hint so that we can ask further questions.

#2: What do you do in your free time?

I love this question, and it is a lot more accurate. Why? Because people can choose what they do in their free time. Want some examples of the answers you might get to this question?

"I love to sing karaoke, dance and act. I love to perform and be around people. Guess I was made to be social." Obviously a blue personality.

"I usually spend quiet evenings at home enjoying my favorite books, surfing the Internet a bit, and doing word puzzles." Okay, an exaggeration, but obviously a green personality.

"Free time! I don't have free time. I am busy working on my career and conquering the world. Did I tell you about all my accomplishments so far this week? And I did all these awesome accomplishments from my new, lavish, seven-bedroom home that has the best home stereo system, the finest masonry … and did I tell you about my art collection? I picked the paintings out personally by outbidding everyone, so that I could take the painting home in my new car …" Yes, we are talking to a red personality who has had too much caffeine.

"I help the local volunteer group raise money to help orphaned puppies find their long-lost fathers. You know, we knit woolen sweaters for these puppies with their own monograms." If you can't tell that this person is a yellow personality, then you probably skimmed this whole book because you are a blue personality. :)

I frequently ask prospects this question: "What do you do in your free time?"

I find their answers interesting, the prospects relax because they know I am truly interested in them, and I also get to understand my prospects better by discovering their underlying color personality.

#3: What do you like most about your job or hobby?

This question exposes people's feelings. And their feelings really show their color personality most accurately. Let me give you an example.

I am standing in line to get my driver's license. After a little conversation with the man in front of me, he tells me that his hobby is making delicious, aromatic gourmet food that is irresistible to animals. So I am thinking, "Wow. That is awesome. He must be a true yellow personality to go through that much effort to bring a little happiness to wildlife."

Then I ask him, "So what do you like most about making gourmet food for wildlife?"

He answers, "It is awesome to see these creatures get suckered in with my food so that I can blast them away with my new high-powered rifle and make more trophies for the wall in my den."

Uh, maybe my prospect isn't a yellow personality after all. By asking this third question, "What do you like most about your hobby?" - I learn his deeper feelings that expose his real color personality.

So when you ask deeper questions, you get closer to the true personalities of your prospects.

See if you can pick out the color personalities from the answers to these questions:

* "I love my job because I meet lots of new people every day."

* "I feel a deep sense of contribution when I help people find the job of their dreams."

* "I love playing this video game because it lets me compete with players all over the world and it posts our scores."

* "I can work on my own. No supervision or distractions. And all I have to do is provide a concise report at the end of the week detailing pertinent information."

The language of colors.

Many times people ask me, "But how can I determine my prospect's personality color over the telephone?"

The answer is easy. Just listen.

Listen for the words your prospect uses to describe what he wants and how he sees the world.

More yellow language.

Let's first consider the words your yellow prospect might use while in conversation with you on the telephone:

Care

Feel

Help

Assist

Mindful

Protect

Anxiety

Concern

Stress

Hardship

Support

Regard

Worry

Polite

Troubling

Bother

Responsible

Safe

Perceive

Sense

Endure

Suffer

Like

Feeling

Consider

Aid

Benefit

Service

Relieve

Heal

Save

Improve

Alleviate

Accommodate

Encourage

Some blue language.

If you are having a telephone conversation with a blue personality (okay, you are just listening and the blue is just talking), you will hear words such as:

Exciting

Fun

New

Travel

Adventure

Awesome

Active

Dynamic

Alive

Keen

Busy

Entertaining

Thrilling

Wonderful

Amazing

Mind-blowing

Dramatic

Buzz

Latest

Different

Trip

Roam

Wander

Risk

Dangerous

Experience

Daredevil

Tour

Explore

Some red language.

If you are having a telephone conversation with a red personality, you will hear words such as:

Power

Control

Compete

Money

Losers

Winners

Authority

Dominate

Drive

Force

Weak

Leverage

Strong

Solid

Helpless

Useless

Command

Manage

Goals

Achieve

Execute

Win

Score

Success

Work

Results

Fail

Wealth

Cash

Profit

Lucrative

Financial

Champion

Conquer

Some green language.

If you are having a telephone conversation with a green personality, you will struggle, since the green will always be checking what you say for accuracy. It is hard to get a green personality to open up and communicate. When the green does speak, you will hear words such as:

Facts

Data

Figures

Information

Security

Research

Proof

Guarantee

Assurance

Commitment

Truth

Certain

Logic

Rely

Statistics

Judgment

Protection

Safe

Evidence

Confirm

Thinking

Common sense

Test

Experiment

Analyze

Examine

Survey

Investigate

Ponder

And even in writing.

Yes, when writing, people will give you hints about their inner personality color. Just read a lengthy email from a yellow and the words of the yellow personality will jump out at you.

Or read the short memo from a red personality and observe all the controlling words and directness.

The better we are at listening and observing, the easier it becomes to distinguish the color personalities of our prospects.

These can be your words, too.

Remember, when you are talking to a prospect who is a different color personality than you, use the words of their language to describe what you are offering.

Don't describe things in your language.

Always describe your offerings in the native language of your prospect.

Do you need to memorize and know all these words? Of course not. They will become obvious in time. But for now, just remember:

Yellows: Help.

Blues: Fun, exciting, adventure.

Reds: Power, results, achieve.

Greens: Information.

That is enough to get you started. Just like learning to drive, the first few days are difficult, but each day things get easier and more automatic.

More on motivating the different color personalities.

As network marketing leaders, motivating our team is important. The ability to motivate people is a measurement of leadership (sounds a bit red, doesn't it?)

One type of motivation doesn't fit everyone. For example, the red leader gives a motivational speech to his team and ends with a challenge to the team by saying:

"I want everyone here to talk to 40 new people tomorrow. I don't care what it takes. Losers have excuses. Winners just … do."

Well, think of the different responses from the team members.

The reds on the team are thinking, "I will talk to **50** new people tomorrow. I am a winner! Look out world, here I come!"

Any blues that were listening will think, "Woo-hoo! Awesome. Talk to more new people. This sounds exciting!"

The yellows are thinking, "Oh, I don't want to do that. I want to build relationships with people. I don't want them to feel just like a number. I am not comfortable with this at all."

And the greens are thinking, "Ridiculous. Talking to 40 new people is like throwing mud on the wall and hoping some of the mud sticks. We need to educate these prospects one-by-one on the benefits of owning their own business. And I am not comfortable accosting strangers on the sidewalk just to meet some artificial number of contacts to satisfy my red leader."

This is why some great contests and motivational campaigns fail. One size doesn't fit all. And maybe one contest or campaign doesn't fit all.

So let's consider how we would motivate each individual color personality, to better understand why not everyone gets motivated the same way we do.

Motivating the yellows.

Will money motivate the yellows? Not really.

What about travel? Well, the yellows are thinking, "Oh who would take care of my cat, Fluffy, while I am gone? And who would talk to my plants? And what would they say?"

Leaving home isn't that motivating to the yellow personality. So let's go back to that key word, "Help."

Yellows will leave their comfort zone to help others. So all you have to say is, "All the profit from our retail sales this month will be donated to orphaned kittens." Now your yellow distributor is a retailing machine. It is easy to talk to strangers to support a bigger cause.

Or maybe an upline leader says, "I just need a few thousand more dollars in volume to make it to Presidential Director." The yellows are the first to purchase more and sell more to help someone else achieve a goal.

Yellow personalities overcome all their fears when the mission is not about themselves. Their mission is to help others.

Yellows also enjoy the concept of community. They love to belong and contribute. Picnics and social events are bonding experiences.

One of the team-building events I have used is holding a potluck dinner. My group would meet in a community hall and distributors would bring a food dish that they had cooked or prepared. Everyone shares and tries each other's food, and it is an inexpensive, enjoyable evening out with friends who have a common interest.

The yellows lived for this event. They loved it. They brought extra food. They brought their friends. And their friends left the dinner with samples, products, and even an audio about the business.

It was easy to invite their friends. No official opportunity meeting, just social, caring people talking about their product experiences, how the extra money helped their lives, and about their dogs and cats.

Having a pot luck dinner every 60 or 90 days guarantees that the yellows will be motivated.

By the way, how do you think the blues felt about the potluck dinner events? Woo-hoo! More people to talk to.

And how do you think the reds felt about these potluck events? (Assuming the reds had feelings … okay, enough red jokes.) Well, the reds hated these events. They would say things such as, "But no one got to see the compensation plan! This needs to be an official meeting with me talking and everyone listening. This social chit-chat is so inefficient."

And how do you think the greens enjoyed these potluck dinners? Ha! Another trick question. The greens didn't come because there were people there!

Motivating the blues.

Easy. When the company announces any travel incentive, the blues are already talking to everyone they know at hyper-speed. They can't wait to go somewhere new and experience new things.

It is not the recognition, and not really about the money, but it is about having fun and excitement.

To a blue, simply say, "We are having a party after the opportunity meeting, just for distributors who bring a guest."

Done.

The blue personality is guaranteed to bring a guest just to be able to attend the party.

They will be saying to strangers, "You've got to join now, and you've got to bring a guest too. We both want to be at that party after the meeting."

If the contest includes international travel, oh my! The blue personalities are the first to run out after the announcement in a frenzy, ready to contact everyone. They will be saying, "You have to join now! We can both qualify. We will fly over on the chartered 747, there will be karaoke on the plane, barrels of iced beer in the aisles, when we arrive we will start taking tours all day, party all night, meet new people, we will stay awake for 72 straight hours, we can be roommates ..." And the blue will hardly mention the company or the products. It is all about the international holiday.

Motivating the reds.

Oh, this is easy. Reds are already self-motivated. They are hard-wired for achievements and results. They love competition. Winning is living.

You can motivate reds simply by listing the top producers in your newsletter or on your webpage. They will constantly be striving to rank higher in the standings.

And, the more positions in your compensation plan, the more chances they have to achieve a higher ranking.

Win a trophy? Of course. The reds believe that the trophy belongs in their home. And what's nice is that every other red on your team believes that trophy belongs in their home also. The reds push each other to higher production and better results.

If there is a trip or holiday to be won, the reds don't really want to go on the trip because that takes time away from building their businesses. However, the reds don't want to be seen as not qualifying, so they excel at almost any incentive.

And don't forget recognition. When the company newsletter features a husband, wife, two children and a dog, posing for their picture in front of the new upscale home with the luxury car in the driveway … you guessed it. This picture is to motivate the reds who read the newsletter.

Every red who sees that picture is thinking, "I wonder how much money they make? I bet I can earn more. And I can earn it faster. I will set the record by earning the luxury car faster."

These vanity pictures are for the reds only. Why? Consider what the other color personalities are thinking when they see that picture.

The yellows are thinking, "Oh, look how she has styled her hair. And their dog looks so lonely. They should get a pet cat so that the dog has a friend."

The blues are thinking, "They are at home! How boring! They need to travel and have fun."

And the greens are thinking, "That luxury car burns so much fuel. My mini-van gets better economy on long trips, plus it has much more storage space."

The reds don't like this.

Do you know a red personality? Would you like to get the red personality in your life to do almost anything you want? It is easy. Just follow this simple formula given to me by Jerry "D'Rhino" Clark.

Step One: Give the red a **compliment**. Of course the red realizes he deserves the compliment.

Step Two: Give the red another **compliment**. Now the red realizes you see his greatness.

Step Three: Give the red a **challenge**. Tell the red there is something you don't think he can do.

Done.

The red can't resist the challenge. The red personality knows you are doing this to him, but he has no defense. His inner red personality won't allow him to fail at the challenge.

Want an example?

"You are the best presenter on my team." (Compliment.)

"And you know more people in the metro area than anyone I know." (Another compliment.)

"**But** Alice sponsored five new distributors last week, and I don't think you could ever beat her record." (Challenge.)"

You can watch the red personality grit his teeth, the blood running to his face, as he thinks, "Alice is going down. I am going to bury Alice. I will sponsor six, seven or even ten people to have that record."

How about another example?

"You are the hardest worker on my team." (Compliment.)

"And nobody is as disciplined as you." (Another compliment.)

"**However**, Alice passed out over 300 catalogs last week while prospecting to get new customers, and I don't think you could ever pass out that many." (Challenge.)

Done.

Next week your red personality will have more than 300 catalogs passed out by mid-week!

Yes, red personalities know you are doing this to them. There is absolutely nothing they can do about it, and they simply must respond to the challenge. This is what green personalities do for fun. They challenge reds all day long just to watch them respond. :)

Motivating the greens.

You are probably scratching your head and thinking, "Gee, how would you motivate a green? I can't think of anything that would work."

And you are right.

You can't motivate the greens. They motivate themselves to take action only after they have accumulated all the information, assimilated all the information, rewritten all the information ... and only then, maybe, take their first baby step towards an action.

Okay, obviously more exaggeration, but it does make it easy to remember. Don't invest a lot of time trying to get greens motivated. Invest that time with motivating the other color personalities. The green personalities are self-motivated, and only at their pace.

Remember, one size doesn't fit all. Different contests or promotions will bring out the best of the different color personalities. And now we understand why some people are excited, and some are not, when a new contest is announced.

Summary.

All the color personalities are good. All the personalities make great leaders.

It doesn't matter what color personality you are. Most of us are born with our personality traits, and there is no need to change them.

So what actually matters?

Our job as communicators is to transfer the message inside of our minds to the minds of others. To be effective, we have to speak in the languages that others understand.

When we observe and recognize the different color personalities, we can choose better words and phrases. This will ensure more accurate communication.

Will everyone we talk to have these exaggerated traits? No. But many will, and with these people, communication will be easy.

So have fun observing people! And get ready for a more enjoyable communication experience.

FREE!

Get 7 mini-reports of amazing, easy sentences that create new, hot prospects.

Discover how just a few correct words can change your network marketing results forever.

Get all seven free Big Al mini-reports, and the free weekly Big Al Report with more recruiting and prospecting tips.

Sign up today at:

http://www.BigAlReport.com

MORE BIG AL RESOURCES

Want Big Al to speak in your area?

Request a Big Al training event:

http://www.BigAlSeminars.com

ABOUT THE AUTHOR

Tom "Big Al" Schreiter has 40+ years of experience in network marketing and MLM. As the author of the original "Big Al" training books in the late '70s, he has continued to speak in over 80 countries on using the exact words and phrases to get prospects to open up their minds and say "YES."

His passion is marketing ideas, marketing campaigns, and how to speak to the subconscious mind in simplified, practical ways. He is always looking for case studies of incredible marketing campaigns that give usable lessons.

As the author of numerous audio trainings, Tom is a favorite speaker at company conventions and regional events.

His blog, **http://www.BigAlBlog.com** is a regular update of network marketing and MLM business-building ideas.

Anyone can subscribe to his free weekly tips at:

http://www.BigAlReport.com

Lightning Source UK Ltd.
Milton Keynes UK
UKOW06f1345140415

249621UK00003B/9/P